Clive Bell

THE FRENCH IMPRESSIONISTS

Φ

Phaidon

PHAIDON PRESS LTD · 5 CROMWELL PLACE · LONDON SW7 2JL

FIRST PUBLISHED 1951

REPRINTED 1961, 1969, 1975

ISBN 0 7148 1206 4

PRINTED IN ITALY

THE FRENCH IMPRESSIONISTS

THE name is too precious to be sacrificed; but 'impressionist', one must admit, is an imprecise description of the group of painters who in 1874 held an exhibition and by a penny-a-liner were dubbed 'Impressionnistes'. They were a mixed lot: some of them were already known as followers of Courbet and Manet, others had worked under the influence of Corot, one at least was a disciple of Ingres. In 1870 they had been more or less independent painters, each going his own way, and ten or twelve years later the best of them were going their own ways again. In the spring of 1874 Manet, who, oddly enough, and for reasons which must be discovered presently, came to be reckoned chief of the band, refused to exhibit with them, only to become a few months later the enthusiastic adept of Pleinairisme, painting under the influence of Monet such admirable impressionist pictures as *Argenteuil*, *La barque*, *Le linge*. And Manet, too, reverted to type. The question remains then: granted that all the painters, with the exception of Manet, included in the present collection took part in the first impressionist exhibition, what else had they in common?

Whatever it may have been, we must seek it between the years 1872 and 1882—the formative and golden decade. There was a doctrine and a technique, both of which will have to be discussed; but not all the impressionist masters believed heartily in the doctrine, and only two practised the technique consistently. Nevertheless, something was held in common, something vaguer but more significant than a doctrine. There was a point of view, an attitude to life and art, which for a time at any rate inspired them all. For a while they shared a new, an essentially 'modern' vision, and a passionate delight therein. Thus they rediscovered Paganism.

> 'The world is so full of a number of things,
>
> I'm sure we should all be as happy as kings.'

That was their discovery. No need for the artist in search of subjects to go to history or mythology or literature; no need to ransack the gorgeous East or the mysterious North; no need to harry a picturesque past in pursuit of fighting Téméraires or stage-coaches or knights in armour; let the artist walk into the street or railway-station or suburban garden, or on to the racecourse, and there he will find beauty galore. Maybe such sentiments sound banal in 1951. They sounded dreadful in the age of Ruskin. They were the ravings of madmen or worse; they stank of anarchy. They were deemed a frontal attack on all that respectable people held sacred. And so they were. For behind these pagan paintings lay an assumption, an assumption that there was no call to worry about the 'Grand-Forever' of respectable church-goers, nor yet about the Welfare State of equally respectable anti-clericals. Without a hope of Heaven or Utopia, life was well worth living for itself and as it was: so it seemed to the Impressionists between 1872 and 1882—in Paris. And yet most of them were very poor.

So far there is something like a common aim or inspiration; and when it came to devising means for expressing this new awareness of the beauty of ordinary sights— of top-hats and four-wheeled cabs, piles of luggage in railway-stations, iron bridges with steam tugs passing under them, embankments and factory chimneys smoking— of everything in fact that mid-century aestheticism considered most inartistic, the Impressionists proper—the Pleinairistes—continued to stick together. Between '72 and '76 (the year of the second exhibition) they evolved a doctrine and a technique. Roughly, the doctrine came to this: if only people would look at what was really there instead of pretending to see the labels imposed on things by the practical intellect or, worse still, by pretentious drawing-masters, they would discover that everything in the garden, or the street, or anywhere else, is lovely—and presumably would buy impressionist pictures. Well, what is *really* there? Light; or, to be subjective, sensations caused by light. So, to render reality, all a painter has to do is to record accurately his visual sensations. Let him take his canvas out of doors and paint what he sees, his visual sensations that is: he will find that colour merges into colour; that bounding lines, like perspective, are mere intellectual makeshifts; that shadows are neither black nor brown but full of a variety of colours; and all will be well. Only let him be true to his sensations and he cannot then be false to visual reality. From this doctrine followed more or less logically the impressionist technique: use of pure colours applied in dots and dashes according to laws which, according to men of science I have met, were imperfectly understood; the division of tones; the juxtaposition of complementaries; the scientific palette in fact. Certain things and practices were anathema, such as mixed colours, colourless shadows, arranged lights and other studio tricks, literature, anecdote and putting in what isn't really there. In theory, impressionist technique was nothing more than a means of recording visual sensations, and impressionist doctrine boils down to this—sensational truth is the only proper study of artists. That, of course, is nonsense, like all exclusive doctrines. Presumably the proper study of artists is to create art. And what is art? Nobody knows. But the doctrine served its turn: it kept at the highest pitch of excitement a group of prodigiously gifted painters who have enriched mankind with enchanting pleasures.

For a few years, between 1872 and 1882 roughly, most of the masters appear to have professed the creed so far as they understood it, though only two practised it consistently. The new wine must have been potent though, to intoxicate Manet, who in August, 1874, when he was forty-two years old and already famous, fell under the spell of Monet—of Monet prime theorist of the movement, faithful to the last—or almost—in theory and practice, too often (alas!) downright doctrinaire. That Manet with his bag of studio-tricks, his name and fame and knack of borrowing from the old masters, should suddenly take his easel out of doors and, sitting beside Monet at Argenteuil, paint what was really there, is convincing evidence of the powerful attraction of Impressionism. It is a case of master turned pupil. To be sure, the sudden conversion was not whole-hearted: there were backslidings; there were nasty bits of work—horrid pastels of fashionable ladies for instance. Still, in 1882 (he died in 1883) Manet finished the *Bar aux Folies-Bergère*, a masterpiece, and, what is to my immediate purpose, an impressionist, though not a pleinairiste, masterpiece. Yet whatever the compelling power of the movement at first, whatever the enthusiasm engendered, by 1882 all the masters were going their own ways. Naturally: great artists—and we are dealing with some of the greatest—are not to be bound by rules and dogmas. They found schools sometimes, they never belong to them. All artists are singular, and—amongst moderns at all events—the greater the more distinct. So let us have done with groups and common characteristics and consider each particular painter represented in this collection. Only allow me to remain in the treacherous world of generalities just long enough to say something about a cleavage in the group itself which in the golden age would seem to have been little understood.

During the last quarter of the nineteenth century and the first few years of the twentieth, the epithet 'impressionist' was employed widely and recklessly. It was used by people whose knowledge of painting was derived mainly from an annual and perfunctory inspection of the rooms at Burlington House to describe any picture that was lively and sincere, or, as they would have said, 'revolutionary'. By similar people it was used also to characterise an argument or stroke at cricket. And even by the cultivated and intelligent a term so popular and so imprecise was applied in places where it had no business. To begin with, it was applied to other arts. The music of Debussy was 'impressionist'; worse still, the prose of the Goncourt journals was 'impressionistic'. Gradually the impressionist painters came to be associated in the public mind with groups of poets and novelists, with playwrights, actors and musicians, with whom all they had in common was a sincere determination to deliver themselves like men of this, the contemporary, world. That the more intelligent and sensitive of the young writers were in sympathy with the impressionist painters goes without saying. Also it should be recorded that they served the movement well: in their early struggles the young painters were helped appreciably by their eloquent allies. But when these allies were called upon to explain exactly what it was they admired in impressionist pictures they found themselves at a loss. Mallarmé, to be sure, could say exquisitely of a landscape by Monet—'C'est aussi expressif que le sourire de la Joconde'; but then, Mallarmé was exceptional. Normal young writers could hardly be expected to do better than discover in these contemporary pictures the qualities they admired in contemporary novels. After all, were they not 'Naturalists' together? So they commended 'psychological subtlety' or 'a sense of man's futility', or 'irony' or 'social criticism' even, qualities which cannot by any stretch of imagination be attributed to landscapes by Monet or Sisley, nor, for that matter, to figures by Renoir or Cézanne, but can, with a little goodwill, be discovered in pictures by Degas and Lautrec, and abundantly in the work of the impressionist illustrators: Forain, Raffaëlli, Steinlen.

The distinction on which I asked leave to insist is now adumbrated. Leaving theory on one side—its proper place—one may say that it was from Corot, Delacroix, Constable, Turner, Courbet and the eighteenth century that the veritable Pleinairistes derived succour. Between 1855 and 1865 Pissarro was in the habit of signing himself 'élève de Corot'. How much Renoir owed to Courbet is apparent, and apparent not only in his early work: what he owed to the eighteenth century he is at no pains to conceal. The Pleinairistes' debt to Turner and Constable has been stated categorically by the Pleinairistes themselves. Now in the productions of those whom I will, for convenience, call 'Naturalists' (Degas, Caillebotte, Lautrec and the Illustrators) I find no response whatever to Corot or Constable. Their masters are Ingres and Japan, and to some extent Manet and Guys; also they have affinities with that school of novelists with whom they share a name. They are modern rather than impressionist. They are not Pleinairistes. Far from seeing the world as Monet saw it, as a congeries of multi-coloured dots and dashes melting into each other, Degas saw it, in the 'seventies and 'eighties, as a pattern—at times a pattern almost flat—consisting of shapes sharply defined. This way of seeing he learnt from Japanese prints. He learnt to describe what he saw from Ingres—a name held in contempt by the more uncompromising Pleinairistes. 'Degas n'est pas assez peintre', said Cézanne, 'il n'a pas assez de ça', sketching that twist of the brush which gives handwriting to a picture. I am not sure that Degas and the Illustrators should be called 'pagan', though I have called them so before now. Raffaëlli was a sentimental Utopist, but Raffaëlli is of small account anyway; Steinlen, who might have been a considerable artist, unluckily insisted on becoming a humanitarian. The fact is, Degas and his followers were not so much in love with the beauty of the world as fascinated by its oddity; and here, you will see, we are coming near the Naturalists of literature—Zola, Edmond de Goncourt, Maupassant. Indeed some of Degas' drawings have the quality of epigrams. Not by going round and about his subject does he record his painfully acute observations, but by telling a simile—*le mot juste*. So, while denying that the art of Degas, or of Lautrec, is literary, we can realise that it would have been far more acceptable to and explicable by contemporary writers than the polychromatic tangles of Monet or Pissarro.

THAT Manet should have been accounted chief of the impressionist school, though he painted only a few impressionist pictures and painted them towards the end of his life, seems odd to us but was, in fact, quite natural. Ever since 1863, the year of the *Déjeuner sur l'herbe* and *Olympia* (not exhibited till 1865), he had been a rallying-point for young and ardent spirits. To them, after Courbet's exile in 1871, he seemed the natural heir, the man who stood for the honour and integrity of art against a world of officials, pot-boilers and prizemen. Certainly he inherited much of the hatred with which these had honoured Courbet, and acquired a fair share on his own account. In the 'sixties he was already well known—'il est plus connu que Garibaldi', sneered Degas. He had money and education. His family was more than respectable; and he dressed and behaved in a manner suitable to his station. Socially he was much above most of his followers, though not above Degas, whose father was always known—quite correctly I believe—as Monsieur de Gas. 'Followers', I said, and I do not think the term excessive, seeing that in 'the seventies' Renoir, Monet, Sisley and the rest, were currently known as '*la bande à Manet*'. Of his late and cursory relations with the school I have already spoken; but, in truth, it is not the paucity of his Impressionism that makes his title surprising, but the fact that at least three of his subordinates were, as artists, infinitely his superiors. Manet painted three or four great pictures but I question whether he was a great painter. Too often there is something common about his art. There was something common about the man. He was consumed by a vulgar ambition for 'honours'—not honour—and praise—not the praise of the few who feel and understand, but of the herd. At heart, I fear, he was what Cézanne would have called a *sale bourgeois*, or perhaps I should say, in one corner of his heart. It is distasteful to think of such a one as 'chief' of Renoir, Cézanne, Degas, Monet, Sisley and Pissarro.

The truth being that there was no chief of the impressionist school, the name of Claude Monet should perhaps head the list. It may be that he and Sisley were the least gifted—and yet how gifted they both were!—of the painters represented in this collection; but certain it is that he and Pissarro were the two who worked out together the theory and practice of Impressionism. And if, as one suspects, Pissarro, who had the better brain, did most of the thinking, Monet was the indefatigable practitioner. At the end of his long life—he died in 1926 at the age of eighty-six—he was an Impressionist still. Before the doctrine had been elaborated, in the 'sixties that is to say, he had painted good pictures under the sway of Boudin and later of Manet and of that ever-to-be-lamented young master, Bazille; he continued to paint good pictures to the end: also, under the influence of theory, he painted some very dull ones—haystacks, cathedrals, views of Westminster. But the work of his life—the forty-odd pictures that compose *Les Nymphéas*—should, in my opinion, be his monument. It is a marvellous achievement and a decoration of the greatest beauty. Why, of the thousands who yearly visit the Orangerie, more do not insist on seeing it, I cannot imagine.

To what extent Renoir was an Impressionist—one who practised what Monet and Pissarro preached—is a question that may be discussed with profit but hardly decided. All that can be said with confidence is that such intimations of Impressionism as are to be found in his work of between 1872 and 1882 had vanished by 1885—the year of *La grande Baignade*. But in that series of pictures which has been called—happily I think—*Scènes de la vie parisienne*, he came as near Impressionism as, given his temperament, refractory to rules and systems, he could come to any 'ism'. This phase of his art, the impressionist or quasi-impressionist, is doubtless the most generally appreciated; and of this phase no works give more delight than *Le Moulin de la Galette*, *La balançoire*, *Les parapluies*, *Déjeuner des canotiers*—scènes de la vie parisienne, in fact. All were painted out of doors, though not *in situ*. Sketches were made on the spot, of course; but, having hired a room with a garden in the half-rustic rue Cortot, Renoir lured thither the pretty girls of the quarter with their dancing partners, and painted them under the trees. There in the blazing summer of 1876 he finished *Le moulin* and *La balançoire*, both of which I am glad to find reproduced in this album. These Parisian pictures are partly impressionist in technique and wholly so in spirit. Here is Naturalism as Renoir understood it: here is the *contemporanéité* of Baudelaire and *le vierge, le vivace et le bel aujourd'hui* of Mallarmé: here is what I have ventured to call the rediscovery of Paganism. No sighing for a better, nobler world here, not yet for 'the breasts of the nymph in the brake'; no imposition of 'the light that never was'; the frocks and faces of shop-girls in sun and shadow, or gas-light for that matter, are quite good enough. Here is Paris in the summer of 1876; what more do you want?

That delicious picture in the National Gallery, *Les parapluies*, is delicious: it is also instructive. It is instructive because it is transitional. Begun, apparently, in 1879, it was finished in the early 'eighties. The two little girls and their pretty mama are still in the impressionist or quasi-impressionist taste, and impressionist is the painting of hair, hats and flowers; but the beautiful midinette shows signs of turning into a goddess, while her band-box is outlined as firmly as it might have been by some great draughtsman who had never heard that lines do not exist in nature. Something had happened; and what had happened—M. Georges Rivière must try to forgive me—was Ingres. Here beginneth the Ingriste period (about 1882–92), and here, so far as Renoir is concerned, Impressionism may be said to end. Look at a photograph—the picture is in America—of *La Grande Baignade* (1885): all the contours are defined by strong lines; tones are not built up in little touches of pure colour but manufactured on the palette; here if anywhere in Renoir's art French girls are turning into fountain statuary of the seventeenth century. (To be sure the little splashing creature remains obstinately in Montmartre.) Compare this picture with a Monet of this or any later period and you will see how far Renoir has travelled from orthodoxy. Truth to tell, there was a radical difference from the first; for while Monet was concerned to render an optical experience, Renoir thought always of making a picture. Making a picture: to that end the genius of the magician was ever bent; to that end his insistence on study in the galleries, and on *métier*; to that end his most telling jest— 'soyez d'abord un bon ouvrier, cela ne vous empêchera pas d'avoir du génie'.

If Renoir was hardly an Impressionist proper, Degas, strictly speaking, was not an Impressionist at all. He was a Naturalist, we have agreed to that; also, in the 'seventies, this devout student of Ingres was probably the most 'modern' painter, alive. In the Japanese print-makers, then becoming fashionable, he had found not matches for his master, but manipulators of form whom he could respect. Indeed, a taste for Japanese prints was one of the few things that all Impressionists— naturalist or pleinairiste—with the possible exception of Renoir—had in common. Degas was a classical draughtsman with a restless modern intellect, and Japan satisfied his taste for modernity without shocking his reverence for line which, as all good Ingristes know, 'est la probité de l'art, est l'honneur même'. But M. Ingres had said nothing memorable about composition; and his own was not of a kind to inspire the highly original genius of Degas. In Japanese prints, on the other hand, he found a hint—and a hint was all his astonishing powers of invention required—to set him off on that method of composition, that way of looking at the subject from odd angles—from right above or just below for instance—which in the 'seventies was deemed a daring novelty and is now become a signature almost. The frankness of Japanese vision, which accepted oddities as a matter of course, suggested to Degas the possibility of making the muzzle of a bassoon or an opera hat, jutting up in front of the proscenium, the foreground of a picture. These fifty years it has been the pastime of tiros to proclaim the debt of Lautrec to Degas: let me urge some mellow critic to compute the debt of Seurat.

The unexpectedness of Degas' designs has been attributed to the study of instantaneous photography. Possibly some were suggested by photographs, but Japanese prints gave him the idea of turning photographs into aesthetically effective patterns. In one sense, however, his art may be called 'instantaneous'; not because

Left: Another way to display orchids—in a still-life composition of flowers, art, and room colors. Here, blue-mauve Vanda Rothschildiana, one of Enid Haupt's favorite orchids, inspired the color of the chair fabric and the collection of ironstone on the dining-room table. Vandas in clay pots are grouped to complement a Cubist painting by Robert Delaunay. Some are underplanted with bromeliads. **Above:** Vanda with Picasso owl plate.

A farmhouse for moderns

Behind a 1790s exterior lies a dazzling remodeling for people who want today's comfort and style

Built in 1790, rebuilt in 1976-77, here's a house that's a paradox. From the road, it seems a nice old New England farmhouse. Inside, it's anything but. When Brian and Marrisa Stone found it, even its timbers were rotted with the sadness of neglect. But they devoted two years to taking down walls, punching in skylights, replacing weak old beams with strong ones from two antique barns they bought for parts, and filling it with everything modern technology and design could devise—all for comfort and quiet in a style all their own.

Left: The living room, with French linen, suedecloth chairs.
Opposite page, left: The garden room, once a lean-to shed, now open to living room.
Below: The dining room— Breuer chairs, French table.

167

Farmhouse for moderns

In the new kitchen professional equipment, skylit eating area, and a Colonial hearth

Above: The kitchen, a room as inviting for its function as for its charm. The glass-doored refrigerator and freezer, like the stove, are restaurant appliances. L-shaped butcher-block counter has marble pastry inset, pull-out leaves. Here, as in the rest of the house, the old windows have been supplemented with skylights (there are 20) and dimmer-controlled lighting. The result is the evenest possible lighting, pierced with spotlights on work areas and art objects.
Right: For old-fashioned warmth, the old fireplace, pine-plank floors.
Opposite page: The kitchen's breakfast area.
Opposite page, bottom: The old American breakfast table, handy to kitchen work area.

ELLIOTT ERWITT

Farmhouse for moderns

The master suite: a bed-sitting room plus a bath equipped like a health spa

The master suite, which takes up half the second floor, includes a huge bed-sitting room and a bath that looks like a health resort. Twenty-five by 14 feet, it's compartmentalized to provide separate areas for a sauna with its own shower, a gym area with professional equipment and a fireplace, an alcove for toilet and bidet, and a main, plank-floored area for the 6-foot-square tub and an extraordinary shower-steam room made of curved glass and fully lined with French tile. The bedroom has a sitting area with a jade green marble mantel, a bar, and a refrigerator.

Left: In the master bath, the huge tub is set in beige marble, as are the double sinks of hand-painted porcelain. Tub has its own hand-shower, and for a faucet, a golden swan.

Opposite page, far left: Skylighted gym (a play area for parents and daughter Sabrina), space-age shower.

Below: Master bedroom, all white, naturals, and beautifully planned comfort. Twelve-foot ceilings are beamed to follow roofline, and five large skylights run nearly the length of the room. Throughout the house, all cabinetry by Peter Luchi; indoor planting by Hal Burke; bath fixtures, Sherle Wagner.

ELLIOTT ERWITT

How to make your luck work for you

By James Austin, M.D.

Of course, we all get lucky sometimes. But there is something to be learned about the structure of chance that may improve your percentage. In the past, the role of sudden flashes of insight in the process of discovery has perhaps been over-emphasized. Much has also been said about the need for plodding, methodical work before and after these creative flashes. But I would like to present the case for chance. What is chance? Dictionaries define chance as something fortuitous that happens unpredictably and without discernible human intention. True, chance is capricious, but we needn't conclude that it is immune from human intervention. Indeed, chance plays several distinct roles when humans react creatively with one another and with their enviroment. I use the word "roles" in the plural because chance comes in four forms and for four different reasons. Of these, only one is "pure blind luck." The principles involved in chance affect everyone and it is time, perhaps, to examine them more carefully. If you are completely candid with yourself you will soon discover how much your luck hinges on contingencies. Every now and then, when you happen to combine boldness and skill, you may be able to exploit a few of the lucky situations that arise. But skill alone will not be enough, for much of the novelty in creativity is decided only when you are bold enough to thrust at chance. "Behold the turtle, he makes progress only when he sticks his neck out," my neurology teacher at Columbia, Professor Houston Merritt used to say. We, too, will only lurch forward if we stick our necks out to look around, and chance the consequences. Our self-mobilization to seek out and confront new situations is a powerful agent in creative discovery. We

all need adventure, and our adventurous impulses may appear in some other form —dreams, for example—if not channeled into our work. For me, research is the essence of adventure. Being a neurologist raised in the conventional work ethic, I still believe that success in research comes from being hard-working, persistent, curious, imaginative, intuitive, and enthusiastic. But it still turns out that many of the lucky breaks in our laboratory are decided by extracurricular activities, by those pivotal events that come only when we have reached out in a spirit of adventure and jousted at chance. Once when we at the lab were trying to identify peculiar microscopic particles in a rare form of hereditary epilepsy called Lafora's disease, my dog, Tom, led us to the answer. Tom developed an inflammation of his lymph glands from wearing a new bell around his neck. After surgery, some of the diseased tissue was studied under a microscope. Curiously, some external tissue showed up as round spherules, first thought to be a fungus but later identified as starch. It got there, we concluded after much discussion, via the starch dusted on the surgical gloves used for the operation. What struck us coincidentally, though, was that the starch spherules looked like the Lafora bodies we were studying! Tests confirmed our hypothesis, and within a few weeks we knew that Lafora bodies, like starch, were essentially made up of many sugar units linked together in a long chain to form a polymer.

In my view, this discovery was a typical case of Chance IV, the variety of chance that favors people with distinctive hobbies and activities (my dog Tom and I go hunting in thick cover, which was the reason I took the precaution of tying the bell around his neck).

Each of the four kinds of chance depends on a distinct kind of motor exploratory activity and special kind of sensory receptivity. Personality traits also influence them.

Continued on page 220

Editor's Note: Dr. James Austin has been involved in brain research for over two decades. For the past ten years he has been Professor and Chairman of the Department of Neurology at the University of Colorado Medical School. In this article, he outlines four categories of luck, a subject he discusses in detail in his forthcoming book Chase, Chance and Creativity, The Lucky Art of Novelty (Columbia University Press, January, 1978, $12.95). The excerpt first appeared in Executive Health Report.

his drawings are like photographs, but because he delights in seizing movement and rendering it in the ungainly exactitude of arrested gesture. Instead of a generalised vision he presents movement petrified. What fascinated him was the character that nature rather than pictorial imagination gives to things. The strangeness of his design is the strangeness of fact; and his genius is the electric spark between an unerring eye and unfaltering finger tips. He caught nature on the hop. In this sense he was instantaneous. And behind the eye, behind photography, behind Japan lay passion— a passion shared by all the best of his generation, by painters, writers and men of science—a passion for truth. This impelled Degas, as it impelled Monet, to see things as they are and not as painters were expected to see them. Also Monet's vision is as truthful as Degas'; for truth, as jesting Pilate knew, is not to be contained in a nut-shell.

I do not think Cézanne ever painted a scientifically impressionist picture. But since during those all-important years 1871 to 1877 he was working with, and almost under the guidance of, Pissarro, and since from Pissarro he learnt lessons that he never forgot, it seems reasonable to reckon him of the school. Besides, he sent pictures to both the eponymous exhibitions: the exhibition of 1874, at which the name was derisively applied, and the exhibition of 1877, at which it was accepted. Anyhow, scholars seem to have decided that from 1872 to 1880 was Cézanne's impressionist period, and that *La maison du pendu* (1874) is an impressionist masterpiece: and who am I to gainsay them? Nevertheless, always there was a profound difference between the impressionist notion of a picture and Cézanne's, a difference which can be demonstrated, mathematically almost, by comparing *Le clos des Mathurins* by Cézanne with *Le clos des Mathurins* by Pissarro. The subject, viewed from different angles, is the same in both, and the pictures are said to have been painted simultaneously. By comparison with Cézanne's severely architectural synthesis, Pissarro's analysis, admirable though it is, appears diffuse, or nearly so. To call it anecdotic would be preposterous; yet it is animated, in the manner of Corot, with a cow, a cowman and a cart, whereas Cézanne's version is austere to the verge of abstraction: some greatly daring critic might find in it a foretaste of Cubism. It was Mr. John Rewald who first struck out this illuminating comparison, so we had better have his words: 'Pissarro's analytical perception,' he says, 'flitting from one detail to another, did not grasp the secret organization of things and landscapes, while, on the contrary, Cézanne's perception unified everything.'

The difference between Cézanne and the other Impressionists is manifest from the first. To begin at the beginning, in the small 'seventies, when the doctrine and technique were being elaborated, whereas most of those who were to become impressionist masters had already given proof of talent and painted good pictures, Cézanne had given proof of little more than temperament and had a shocking pictorial past to live down. For, in the 'sixties, this fiery but feeble young poet turned painter, his temper inflamed—one would hesitate to say influenced—by Delacroix and Courbet, had dreamed of inventing plastic equivalents for his melodramatic imaginings. Far from recording visual sensations, he was resolved to write tragedies and satires in paint. The results were not encouraging: and in 1870 no critic could have recognised in the works of what Cézanne himself called his *couillarde* manner the *juvenilia* of a master. In Paris, even to benevolent acquaintances—though not, I think, to Pissarro—he probably appeared an uncouth and ungifted hanger-on to *la bande à Manet*. So, in the early years of Impressionism, he had to learn, not only to paint, but to master his emotions. Much he learnt from Manet, whom he did not love, and more from Pissarro, whom no one could help respecting. He learnt to keep his eye on the subject and to eschew rhetoric. By 1880 or so he had learnt all the Impressionists had to teach. Indeed by 1877—the latest admissible date for *Le clos des Mathurins*—it looks as though Cézanne were already dreaming of making of Impressionism 'quelque chose de solide et de durable comme l'art des musées'. That dream came true. About 1882 begins the classical period, the serene years of calm creation, the years during which were to be produced some of the supreme triumphs of modern painting. Into that period it is no business of a commentator on Impressionism to pry.

Of the great Impressionists, Sisley is probably the least admired; Pissarro, in my opinion, is the most under-rated. That Sisley, born of English parents in Paris, was an exquisite painter is freely admitted, but one has only to look at his *Inondation* in the Jeu de Paume to feel that he was something more. Seeing that he was in London with Monet in 1871, and that together they discovered Turner—and doubtless Constable—one may assume he played some part in the formation of Impressionism. But Sisley was no theorist, which does not matter, and no taker of Heaven by storm, which does. That matters, because in middle age he sometimes thought it his duty to attempt the feat. Inevitably he failed and his failures are not very interesting. He was a poet—an English poet—with delicate perceptions of, and reactions to, the moods of nature. When he allows these to choose his theme and guide his hand he is at his best; when he tries to be a little strong he is a little unsatisfactory. Had he lived longer—he died before he was sixty—he would have painted more good pictures; I do not think he would have painted better ones or different.

How unlike that is the case of Pissarro! With his strong, inquisitive mind he was a born explorer. Certainly he was an Impressionist to the end of his days; but he was not an Impressionist every day. Never content to rest under his laurels, green and flourishing though they were, he kept an eye on what Signac and Seurat were about, and on Maurice Denis and Gauguin too. There might be something in any new theory, and he was not going to dismiss it till he had explored its possibilities. This open-mindedness and taste for experiment, admirable in themselves, seem—strange to say—in no way to have debilitated the artist's personality. On the contrary, his art was enriched by his researches. Pissarro was a thorough good painter from first to last; and each picture of his that I see persuades me that he is better than I had supposed. Mauclair, to be sure, ranks him with 'the secondary painters of Impressionism', along with Sisley, Bazille and Cézanne: for my part, I am sometimes tempted to rank him with the very greatest—a temptation to be resisted no doubt. But the term 'secondary' I find hard to swallow: Pissarro is first-rate. Make this experiment: upstairs in the Jeu de Paume hangs a landscape—I will allow explorers the fun of discovering it for themselves; ignore the writing on the frame and ask yourself whether you might not have taken it for a Cézanne, and a good Cézanne. The picture is by Pissarro: it is in no sense an imitation—quite the reverse.

There was a respectable second generation of Impressionists: Impressionism is the one school of the nineteenth century which can boast so much continuity. It should not be forgotten—though often it is—that Gauguin, Seurat and Redon all sent pictures to the later exhibitions: Gauguin, for that matter, learnt what he knew of the art of painting from Pissarro. As for Lautrec, if we are not to call this direct descendant of Degas a 'Naturalist' what are we to call Degas himself? But, besides this younger generation of masters, there were plenty of good painters, born too late to participate in the Impressionist Exhibitions—the last was held in 1886—who yet derived their science and point of view from the movement. The young Sickert—more than a good painter, manifestly a young master—and the young Steer, the

Canadian J. W. Morrice and possibly Conder, may all, I think, be reckoned inheritors of the tradition. And then there are minor but far from negligible artists of the first and second generations, for whom obviously no place could be found in this album, who yet deserve notice and perhaps a volume to themselves. There is Berthe Morisot, an original member of the group and almost one of the great; there are Lépine, Lebourg, Signac, Cross, Mary Cassatt, Nittis, Meteyard, Vignon, Loiseau: something could be said for all these, and for a dozen more, and I wish someone would say it. I wish someone would trace the ramifications of the movement in England, Scotland, America and elsewhere, and attempt to define the boundaries of impressionist influence not only in space but in time. Though to us Bonnard and Vuillard may seem to inhabit a world of their own, I am not sure that future historians will accept our view. After all, the most potent forces in their development were Japan, Degas and Gauguin. A hundred years hence Bonnard and Vuillard may be called the last of the Impressionists. 'One can believe anything of the future' said Sir Max Beerbohm: the historian may go further still. As likely as not he will claim Fauvism as the last chapter in the story, and make of Matisse its 'explicit'. I can foresee the argument, and it is tenable. The Impressionists, he will say, though they painted nothing but what they saw, were the first to break with the Renaissance tradition. Ever since the Renaissance, and for hundreds of years before, visual artists had sought a compromise between what they saw and what the grocer thinks he sees (under the honourable style of 'grocer' I subsume the nobility and gentry, merchants and artisans, the law, the church and the armed forces). The Impressionists were the first—with the exception of Turner in his old age—to be quite uncompromising. What they painted was not in the least like what the grocer thought he saw. All grocerdom screamed. When it had done screaming it acquiesced. Henceforth it was agreed that Art and what the grocer thinks he sees are two quite different things. 'And so,' says the triumphant but unborn historian, 'Impressionism leads straight to Picasso.'

LIST OF PLATES

LIST OF PLATES

Our thanks are due to all who have kindly agreed to the reproduction of paintings in their possession, especially to M. Durand-Ruel and M. Philippe Gangnat, and the Trustees of the Tate Gallery.

REPRODUCTION RÉSERVÉE
SYNDICAT DE LA PROPRIÉTÉ ARTISTIQUE
PARIS

1. ÉDOUARD MANET. PORTRAIT DE ZOLA

PORTRAIT OF ZOLA

2. ÉDOUARD MANET. LE DÉJEUNER SUR L'HERBE · THE PICNIC

4. ÉDOUARD MANET. FEMME NUE EN BUSTE

NUDE

5. ÉDOUARD MANET. BERTHE MORISOT AU CHAPEAU NOIR   BERTHE MORISOT IN A BLACK HAT

6. ÉDOUARD MANET. LE BALCON   THE BALCONY

7. ÉDOUARD MANET. ARGENTEUIL

VIEW OF ARGENTEUIL

8. ÉDOUARD MANET. LA BARQUE DE MONET

9. CLAUDE MONET. LA PLAGE DE TROUVILLE

10. CLAUDE MONET. Mme MONET ET BAZILLE AU JARDIN   Mme MONET AND BAZILLE IN THE GARDEN

11. CLAUDE MONET. FEMMES AU JARDIN   LADIES IN THE GARDEN

12. CLAUDE MONET. IMPRESSION DE SOLEIL COUCHANT

14. CLAUDE MONET. LA CHARRETTE, ROUTE D'HONFLEUR

15. CLAUDE MONET. LA GARE SAINT-LAZARE

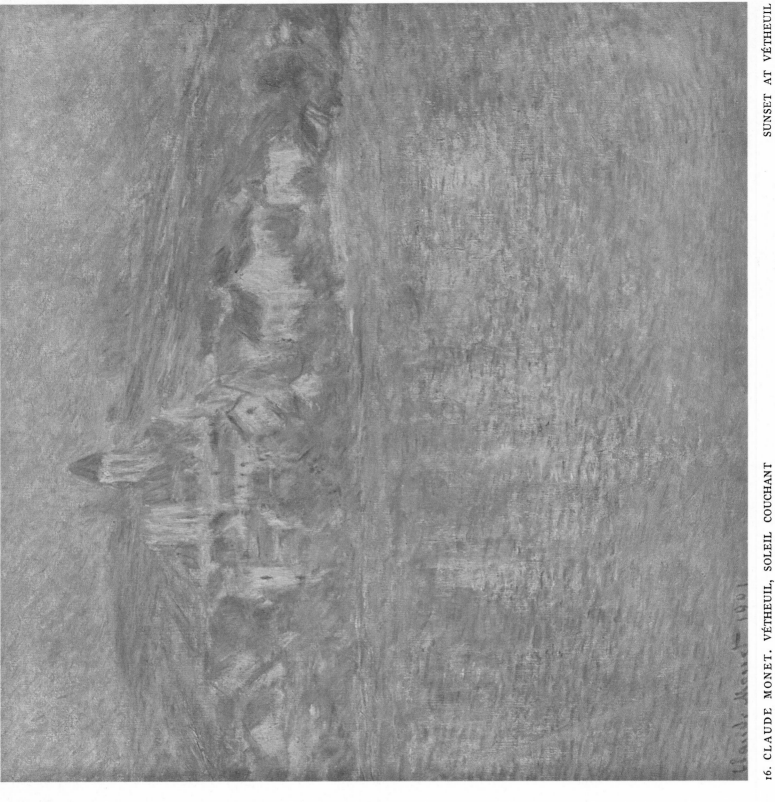

16. CLAUDE MONET. VÉTHEUIL, SOLEIL COUCHANT

18. ALFRED SISLEY. RÉGATES PRÈS DE LONDRES

REGATTA ON THE THAMES

19. ALFRED SISLEY. LA BARQUE PENDANT L'INONDATION

FLOODS AT PORT-MARLY

20. ALFRED SISLEY. LA PASSERELLE D'ARGENTEUIL   FOOTBRIDGE NEAR ARGENTEUIL

21. ALFRED SISLEY. EFFET DE NEIGE, LE CHASSEUR   SNOWSCAPE WITH HUNTSMAN

22. CAMILLE PISSARRO. JEUNE FILLE A LA BAGUETTE   GIRL WITH A SWITCH

23. CAMILLE PISSARRO. FEMME DANS UN CLOS

24. CAMILLE PISSARRO. ROUEN, SOLEIL COUCHANT

25. CAMILLE PISSARRO. LA FEMME AU BONNET ROUGE   WOMAN WITH RED KERCHIEF

26. PAUL CÉZANNE. PORTRAIT DE L'ARTISTE   SELF-PORTRAIT

27. PAUL CÉZANNE. PEUPLIERS

29. PAUL CÉZANNE. NATURE MORTE AU PANIER

31. PAUL CÉZANNE. LA VALLÉE DE L'ARC   THE ARC VALLEY

32. PAUL CÉZANNE. JEUNE ITALIENNE

ITALIAN GIRL

33. PAUL CÉZANNE. LA VIEILLE AU CHAPELET   OLD WOMAN WITH ROSARY

34. EDGAR DEGAS. L'ABSINTHE

IN THE CAFÉ

35. EDGAR DEGAS. MUSICIENS A L'ORCHESTRE   THE ORCHESTRA OF THE PARIS OPERA

36. EDGAR DEGAS. FIN D'ARABESQUE   CLOSE OF AN ARABESQUE

39. EDGAR DEGAS. APRÈS LE BAIN · · · · · · · · · · · · · AFTER THE BATH

40. EDGAR DEGAS. DANSEUSES

BALLET DANCERS

41. AUGUSTE RENOIR. Mᵐᵉ MONET ET SON FILS

43. AUGUSTE RENOIR. LA BALANÇOIRE

THE SWING

44. AUGUSTE RENOIR. Mlle GRIMPEL AU RUBAN BLEU   Mlle GRIMPEL WITH A BLUE RIBBON

45. AUGUSTE RENOIR. JEUNE FEMME AU FOND BLEU   YOUNG WOMAN ON BLUE BACKGROUND

46. AUGUSTE RENOIR. NU

SEATED NUDE

47. AUGUSTE RENOIR. COCO ÉCRIVANT   COCO, THE ARTIST'S SON, WRITING

48. AUGUSTE RENOIR. COCO ET LES DEUX SERVANTES   COCO, THE ARTIST'S SON, AND TWO SERVANTS

49. AUGUSTE RENOIR. PAYSAGE BLEU   BLUE LANDSCAPE

50. AUGUSTE RENOIR. FRAISES   STILL-LIFE WITH STRAWBERRIES